JOEY

The Story of a Baby Kangaroo

WRITTEN AND PHOTOGRAPHED BY

HOPE RYDEN

TAMBOURINE BOOKS NEW YORK

Library of Congress Cataloging in Publication Data

Ryden, Hope. Joey: the story of a baby kangaroo/by Hope Ryden.—1st ed. p. cm. Summary: Follows a baby

kangaroo, or joey, as it grows inside its mother's pouch and learns about the other animals living on Australia's

Kangaroo Island. 1. Kangaroos—Infancy—Juvenile literature. 2. Macropus fuliginosus—Juvenile literature. [1.

Kangaroos. 2. Animals—Infancy.] I. Title. QL737.M35R93 1994   599.2—dc20   93-15419 CIP AC

ISBN 0-688-12744-4. — ISBN 0-688-12745-2 (lib. bdg.)

First Edition 10 9 8 7 6 5 4 3 2 1

For my nature-loving husband, John,
who shared my astonishment at the wonders of Australia.

A baby kangaroo lived in a scrub forest in Australia. Most of the time he lay cradled in a pouch on his mother's belly. Sometimes when the sun was shining, he stuck his head out.

A koala watched the mother and baby. He was glad to see them hop away. He didn't like company— not even the company of other koalas. He preferred to be by himself in a tree and eat eucalyptus leaves.

The baby kangaroo had lived in his mother's pouch since he was three quarters of an inch long. Soon after his birth he had crawled there. At first all he did was sleep and suckle his mother's milk. As he grew bigger, he began to stick his head out and sample plants.

A baby kangaroo is called a joey. By the time this joey was seven months old, he could step out of the pouch whenever he wanted to.

It felt good to hop around and have a stretch. Riding in a pouch all the time was pretty confining.

What's more, there wasn't much room inside the pouch to groom himself or scratch where it itched.

The best part of being outside, though, was seeing his
mother's face...

and nuzzling her ear. Like most baby animals, he was very
attached to his mother.

When he grew tired, he crawled back into the pouch. Then his mother closed the opening as easily as if it were a drawstring purse. It was dark and safe inside.

While her joey slept inside her pouch, the mother kangaroo mingled with others of her kind. She was sociable by nature. Not all of the many kinds of kangaroos that live in Australia are. Some are loners.

Often she was joined by her last year's baby. He was now
half grown and almost independent. Still, he had not yet
broken all ties with his mother.

Sometimes the two of them set off together to find good grass. Of course the new joey came along, too— asleep in his mother's pouch. On the road they met other animals.

Once they came upon a sand goanna. A sand goanna is a very large Australian lizard that feeds on birds and insects.

Another time they met an echidna. An echidna looks dangerous, but it has no teeth. Echidnas eat ants and termites, which they catch with their long, sticky tongues. When faced with danger, they roll up into tight, spiky balls.

When the baby joey wasn't sleeping, he climbed out of the pouch and played with his half-grown brother. Their mother looked on while her two youngsters boxed.

Every day the baby joey grew a little. And every day he learned something new. He was very curious and watched what his mother did.

He noticed other animals that lived in his habitat too. One day he saw an emu.

The emu looked fierce. It was taller than the joey's mother. It had eyes as red as rubies. It looked like it could pick up a baby kangaroo and fly away with him!

In one hop the joey dived headfirst into his mother's pouch.
He didn't know that emus don't attack baby kangaroos.
Emus can't even fly! Although he was growing bigger every
day, this joey had much to learn.

He needed to grow stronger too. Some nights he play-boxed with his mother. This helped him to develop fighting skills. As a grown-up, he would have to box in earnest with other adult males.

He also needed to be alert for danger—especially the presence of dingoes.

Dingoes are wild dogs that live in Australia. Dingoes are predators. Unlike kangaroos, they cannot make a meal of grass. They must eat meat. So sometimes they kill kangaroos for food.

Other predators lived in the kangaroo habitat too. At night a tiger quoll came out to hunt. But this animal was no threat to the little joey. It preyed on small animals...

such as this fat-tailed dunnart. Fat-tailed dunnarts eat grasshoppers. When they've feasted on more than they need their tails get fat.

As time passed many rains fell. The grass that grew on the fringe of the forest got long. The baby kangaroo learned to eat this lush food. Soon he became almost too big and too heavy for his mother to carry in her pouch.

But this joey was not yet ready to be on his own. He still needed care and affection. Nor was his mother ready to let him go. She still liked to play with him.

And so he continued to drink milk from her nipple, which was located inside her pouch.

Getting all the way in, however, was becoming a problem.

Whenever he took a nap his legs and head stuck out.

And if his mother wanted to hop to a new place she had to tuck him in.

Carrying such a heavy
joey slowed her down.

Should a pack of dingoes take off after her, the mother kangaroo might not be able to outdistance them.

Besides, this joey didn't really need to be carried around anymore. Couldn't he hop almost as fast and far as his mother?

Like it or not, the time had come for him to travel about on his own two feet. More important, something new had happened. Although he didn't know it yet, a newborn baby had taken over his mother's pouch. Now *he* was the big brother!

More About Kangaroos

Kangaroos are found only in Australia and nearby New Guinea. Millions of years ago these two places were joined, and the animals that arose on that ancient land mass were special in many ways. For example, a baby kangaroo is less than an inch long at birth and is so undeveloped that it looks more like a grub worm than a warm-blooded animal. It has no hair, and its eyes, ears, and hind legs are only partly formed. Even so it manages to make its way through its mother's fur to her pouch opening and crawl inside. Once there it takes hold of a teat and begins suckling milk. For several months it remains attached to that teat while it continues to develop into a completed baby. Not until its hind legs have formed and its eyes and ears have opened does it begin to poke its head out of the pouch opening and look around—like the joey in this book.

There are fifty-two kinds of kangaroos in Australia and New Guinea. Some are classified as wallabies. Others are called wallaroos. The smallest member of this interesting family is called a potoroo. It is no bigger than a guinea pig. The largest member is the red kangaroo. Male reds measure eight feet from nose to tail tip. Some species of kangaroos live in trees. Others live on rocky slopes. Still others make their homes in deserts. The kangaroos in this book choose to live in and around scrub forests on an off-shore island. They are commonly called Kangaroo Island kangaroos. On the mainland this animal is known as the western grey kangaroo. It has a scientific name, too—*Macropus fuliginosus*.

Macropus fuliginosus is a sociable species, especially the females. The males also like company, but they are bigger and more aggressive than the females and sometimes get into fights. During these contests two males will pummel each other's heads with their front paws. They will also deliver kicks to each other's bellies with their powerful hind feet.

Kangaroos are not the only animals in Australia that give birth to unfinished offspring and then carry them around in their pouches. One hundred and twenty species, including koalas and tiger quolls, do the same. Scientists call all such animals marsupials.

Pronunciation Guide

Dunnart	(DONE-ert)
Echidna	(eh-KID-nuh)
Emu	(EE-mew)
Eucalyptus	(you-kuh-LIP-tuss)
Goanna	(go-WAH-nuh)
Koala	(kuh-WAH-lah)
Marsupial	(mar-SOUP-ee-ull)
Potoroo	(PO-tuh-roo)
Quoll	(kwole)
Wallaby	(WALL-uh-bee)
Wallaroo	(WALL-uh-roo)